Sweet Marjoram

Parsley

Thyme

Sage

Rosemary

My Own Herb Garden

My Own Herb Garden

by *Allan A. Swenson*

Illustrated by Allianora Rosse

Rodale Press, Inc. Book Division, Emmaus, Pennsylvania 18049

Library of Congress Cataloging in Publication Data

Swenson, Allan A.
  My own herb garden.

  Includes index.
  SUMMARY: Explains how to plan, plant, and care
for an indoor or outdoor herb garden with specific
instructions for growing ten herbs.
    1. Herb gardening—Juvenile literature.
2. Organic gardening—Juvenile literature.
[1. Herb gardening. 2. Gardening] I. Rosse,
Allianora. II. Title.
SB351.H5S93   635´.7´0973   76–3326
ISBN 0–87857–129–9

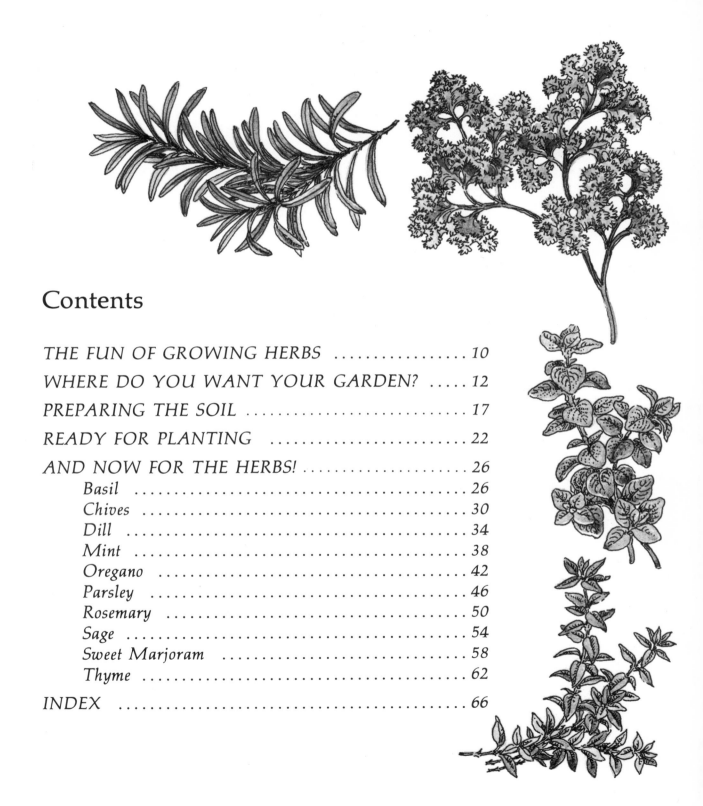

Contents

THE FUN OF GROWING HERBS

A bag of
dried herbs makes
a nice gift.

Herbs are easy to grow. They are hardy and don't require very much care. They're also nice to look at.

Many herbs bear beautiful blossoms. Others add fragrance to gardens and rooms.

But the best thing about herbs is their flavor. Even a small pinch of one herb or a leaf of another can make meals come alive with delightful new taste treats.

You can sprinkle herbs on salads or add them to soup.

You can blend them with vegetables or into gravy or sauces. You can cook them to season meat.

Some herbs, like parsley and mint, add beauty as well as flavor to food.

And you can grow herbs yourself in a garden of your very own, either indoors or outdoors.

If you're a beginning gardener, however, you will probably want some help from your parents, or perhaps an older brother or sister, especially if you decide to have an outdoor garden. So an herb garden can be a family project as well as something very special of your own. And everyone in your family, of course, will enjoy the herbs you grow.

Another nice thing about herbs is that you can enjoy them year-round, unlike most other food plants that are harvested just one time or only during the summer. Once your herbs are mature, you can snip off a piece any time you want some special flavoring.

A sprig of mint makes
lemonade taste better.

There are many types of herbs. Beginning on page 26 you will find pictures of ten favorite herbs you can grow, plus interesting things about them and how to plant, care for, and use each one.

You may want to grow some of the herbs indoors in pots in a little window garden.

Others you may want to grow in planters or tubs on the patio or outside your kitchen door.

Still others you can grow in your own special plot in your family's vegetable garden, or as a border around flowers, or along a path or walkway.

Some herbs grow for just one season. These are called *annuals.* Herbs that are planted once and keep sending up new plants every year are called *perennials.* And herbs that are planted in one season and do not bloom until the following season are called *biennials.*

In this book you will discover many ways and places to grow herbs successfully and easily. Just as exciting, you'll learn how you can use your herbs every day for almost every meal, if you wish.

But even though herbs are easy to grow, there are right ways and wrong ways to go about it, just as with everything else. So the more you know about growing herbs, the more successful your herb garden will be.

We'll tell you all about pots and planters, about soil and fertilizers, and about how to plant and harvest herbs.

Now, if you want to know how to start planning and planting your very own herb garden, just turn the page.

Basil adds special flavor to tomatoes.

Chives ready for cutting.

A windowsill
herb garden.

WHERE DO YOU WANT YOUR GARDEN?

Some herbs like lots of sun; others like shadier areas. Later on, when we talk about each herb, we will tell you which each one prefers.

But for now, just remember that you can grow all the herbs in this book either indoors or outdoors.

Indoor Garden

What You Will Need

If you decide to start an indoor herb garden, there are three basic things you will need:

1. *Pots.* You may not know it, but you probably have all kinds of "pots" around your house. Empty cottage-cheese containers or decorative margarine tubs can make suitable pots for growing herbs. Be sure to wash them thoroughly before using. If you wish, however, you can buy pots wherever garden supplies are sold.

Some gardeners prefer clay pots. But clay pots can break, and you can use plastic pots just as well.

12

If you already have some clay pots, of course, you can certainly use these for your herbs. If they have had soil in them before, scrub them out well with hot water and soap or detergent and rinse.

2. *Pebbles or Gravel.* Whichever kind of pot you use, put a base of small stones or pebbles in the bottom of each pot before you fill it with soil. You can also use gravel, which you might be able to find outside. Or you can break a damaged clay pot into small pieces and use some of these as your base.

Put about ½ inch of pebbles or gravel or bits of clay pot in the small pots you plan to use. For pots that are 8 inches or more in diameter, increase the amount of pebbles or gravel to about 1 inch.

3. *Trays or Pans.* You can put your pots on saucers right on a windowsill if it is wide enough. If not, use a table or stand in front of the window.

An even better idea is to place your pots on a tray that has a layer of pebbles or gravel in it. This will keep your window garden looking neat and will help contain accidental spills when you water your herbs.

Herbs, like most other plants, don't welcome wet "feet." Too much water can actually rot their roots. When that happens, food nutrients in the soil have no way of getting up into the stems and leaves.

Garden centers sell many types of trays. But you don't have to buy a special tray if you have a large baking pan or cookie tin. Or you may want to use an aluminum foil pie pan as an individual tray for each potted herb.

Pieces of an old clay pot make a good base.

Saucers, pie tins or a tray under plants keep a windowsill garden neat.

Choosing a Location

A good growing place for most herbs indoors is in a window that faces south. But if the south windows in your house are shaded by tall trees or buildings, windows that face east are also good for most herbs.

Caution: If the window you select gets intense sun or heat at times during the day, be sure to keep the pots back from the glass panes so your plants won't get burned.

And never put plants on top of a hot radiator.

Basil

Sage

Dill

Mint

Marjoram

Sweet Basil

Sage seedlings

Chives

Outdoor Garden

Where to Plant

Pick a sunny location for herbs that thrive in sun. Select a more shaded spot for those that like only partial sun.

Rule of green thumb: Sun-loving herbs should get 5 to 8 hours or more of sun each day. Those that prefer partial sun or partial shade need 3 to 5 hours of sun.

Ways to Plant

One of the nice things about growing herbs outdoors is that there are many ways you can plant them.

You can, of course, plant herbs right in the ground in beds or rows in your own outdoor garden. You can plant them as a border around a flower bed, or in a rock garden, or along a path. You can plant different herbs in sections in a wagon-wheel arrangement.

The illustration below shows you how to make a circle and divide it into equal sections for a "wagon-wheel" garden.

With two pointed sticks and a piece of string you can make a perfect circle. Then divide it into sections for a "wagon-wheel" garden.

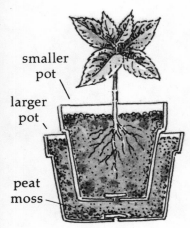

smaller pot

larger pot

peat moss

Outdoor Planters

If you don't have a yard or enough room for a regular garden, you can still grow herbs outdoors in pots or planters on a patio or porch.

There are many different types of planters. Some are made of redwood in box or tub shapes. Or you can use a large metal tub or bucket.

Another method is to put a pot inside a pot. This is called double-potting.

Just put the pot in which you have planted your herb inside a larger container. If you use a clay inner pot, fill the space between the two pots with soil or peat moss. That will keep the moisture in the clay pot from drying out. You can get packaged peat moss in garden stores or in five-and-dime variety stores.

Another method is to grow herbs in cinderblock planters. Either sink the blocks in holes in the ground or place them on top of the ground where you want them. Then fill the empty spaces with soil and plant your herbs.

If you live where winters get cold, an even better idea is to grow herbs in pots sunk in the ground. Then when frost threatens, you can simply dig them up, pots and all, and bring them indoors for the winter.

cinderblock planter

Movable Herbs

Indoors or outdoors, the big advantage of growing herbs in pots or planters is that you have "portable plants."

You can place them anywhere you like as long as they can get the sun or shade they need.

pots sunk in the ground

16

PREPARING THE SOIL

Along with sunlight and water, herbs need good soil to grow strong and healthy.

Indoor Garden

Soil You Can Mix Yourself

There are many places you can find soil for your potted herbs.

Maybe your father or mother already has an outdoor garden, and you can use some soil from that. Or perhaps a neighbor has a garden and will let you have some topsoil. You really won't need very much.

Topsoil is the first few inches of earth. Good topsoil is crumbly. You should be able to break it up with your fingers. Don't use soil that is hard or sticky with clay. The soil should also be as free as possible from stones or roots.

To make a good potting-soil mix:

1. Start with a bucket about ⅓ full of soil.

2. Add equal parts of sand and peat moss—that is, ⅓ soil, ⅓ sand, and ⅓ peat moss. You can buy peat moss in a garden center or a variety store.

If you have an old sandpile, or know of one nearby, you can use this sand. Or perhaps a new house is being built in your neighborhood, and the builder will let you have some sand.

Be sure the sand you use is coarse rather than very fine. Coarse sand mixes better with soil and helps the soil hold moisture.

soil

sand   peat moss

Instead of peat moss, you can also use humus from the woods. Nature makes this humus from decaying leaves and plants. (This is also called "compost." Later we will tell you how you can make your own.)

3. Mix the soil, sand, and peat moss (or humus) in the bucket. Stir well, using your hands or a large spoon, because the roots of your herbs will be growing all through this mixture.

4. Now put the soil in the pots you have ready. Fill the pots loosely, to about 1 inch from the top. Don't pack or tamp the mixture down tightly.

As you fill each pot, mix in 1 or 2 teaspoonfuls of bonemeal, depending upon the size of the pot.

Bonemeal is made from the bones of animals and contains food nutrients plants need. You can buy bonemeal at a garden center or a variety store. A small package of bonemeal will last a long time.

Soil You Can Buy

Many stores sell potting soil already prepared for house plants.

This soil is good for herbs, too, because it usually has a number of ingredients in it to encourage plant growth. It has also been sterilized to kill anything that might be harmful to plants.

Packaged potting soil is especially convenient if you live in a city apartment and cannot simply run outside and dig up your own! It comes in different sizes of packages, so you can buy only as much as you need.

It's still a good idea, however, to mix a little bonemeal in with the potting soil as you fill your pots.

Top layer: leaves and sticks
Middle layer: decaying leaves and sticks
Bottom layer: humus

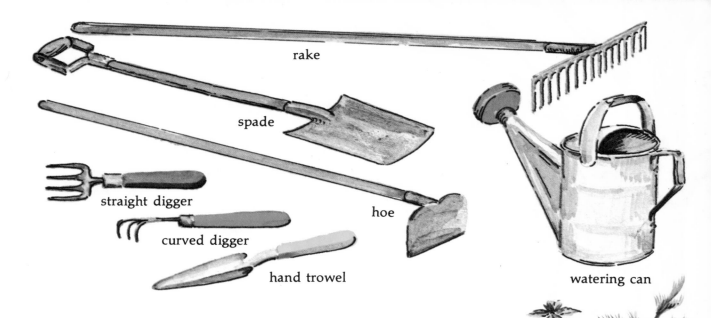

rake

spade

straight digger

curved digger

hoe

hand trowel

watering can

Outdoor Garden

Tools You Will Need

A spade, a rake, a hand trowel, and a digger are your basic outdoor gardening tools.

You should also have a long-necked watering can with a sprinkling head. This helps distribute water evenly and gently. A strong stream of water digs holes around plants, and sometimes washes away seeds.

Getting the Ground Ready

Herbs tend to send down deep roots. Because of this, if you want your herbs to grow properly, the soil you plant them in should not be hard or packed.

This isn't a problem if you use pots sunk in the ground or cinderblocks or raised beds or sections, as in the wagon-wheel arrangement. In these cases, you will be filling the growing spaces with soil that has already been broken up.

19

Dig deep.

Turn soil over.

Rake lightly before planting.

Add mulch around plants.

But if you plan on having a regular row garden, it may take some digging to get the ground ready, especially if it hasn't been used for a garden before. This is another way you can get the whole family involved in your herb garden.

These days, more and more people are growing their own vegetables. If your parents are planning a vegetable garden, suggest that they reserve a small area for your herbs. This way, everybody can pitch in and get the necessary digging done at one time.

The important thing to remember is that the soil must be well spaded. Dig down to about the depth of your spade. As you turn the clumps over and break them up, mix in compost or humus. Peat moss is also good. These substances will not only add nutrients to the soil but will also help keep it loose and porous.

After you plant your herbs, the next thing you should do is to mulch. Mulching is simply a way to protect your seeds or plants. You can use compost, peat moss, or straw, or almost any kind of shredded plant material as a mulch. Just spread it on the ground around your plants.

The mulch will discourage weeds, and as rain falls or you water your plants, additional nutrients from the mulch will soak into the ground and feed the roots.

What Fertilizer Is and Does

Fertilizer is many things. It is compost or humus. It is manure. It is bonemeal. It is everything that contains elements plants need to grow.

Think of fertilizer as food—food for your plants.

Fertilizers that are made from once-living plants or

20

the products of animals are called "organic" fertilizers.

The most important elements in fertilizers are nitrogen, phosphorous, and potash (or potassium). Plants must have these elements to grow roots, stems, and leaves. Natural feeding with organic fertilizers will give your herbs the nutrients they need. Soil that contains all these nutrients is called "rich" soil.

You can buy a variety of organic fertilizers. But it is easy to make your own in a compost pile.

How to Make Compost

Every bit of once-living plant material—leaves, grass clippings, straw, even sawdust—is useful to feed other plants. All are organic materials. When they decay and rot down, they provide nutrients for growing plants.

Organic material that is well decayed, or composted, is called humus.

The easiest way to make compost is simply to gather leaves and grass clippings in a pile. You can add vegetable scraps from the kitchen (but not meat or grease). Keep out branches or sticks or other hard materials.

Keep the compost pile moist.

Set the whole family to building the compost pile. The more contributions the better. Then moisten and turn the pile regularly, about every few days.

Bacteria—tiny organisms so small they can't be seen except with a microscope—will go to work on the organic material. In a few weeks it will turn into rich, dark humus that will supply your plants with the food they need.

Then you can use the humus to prepare potting mixes for your indoor garden. Outdoors, you can use it both as fertilizer and as a top-dressing, or mulch.

21

READY FOR PLANTING

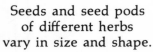

starting with seeds

Your garden is well spaded and fertilized. Or your pots are filled with potting mix. You're ready to start growing herbs.

Now the question is, which shall you use: seeds, seedlings, cuttings, or transplants?

When we discuss each individual herb in the next chapter, we will tell you which method is best for that herb. But here are a few general instructions.

Three Ways to Start Your Garden

Seeds

All the herbs in this book can be started from seeds, and this is probably the method you will decide to use.

Growing herbs from seeds is really fun because you can watch your plants develop from the beginning. Just be sure not to plant seeds too deeply.

Seeds are small. Stored inside them is a food supply to get the plants started, but once the plants sprout, roots reach down to obtain food from the soil.

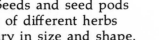

Seeds and seed pods
of different herbs
vary in size and shape.

22

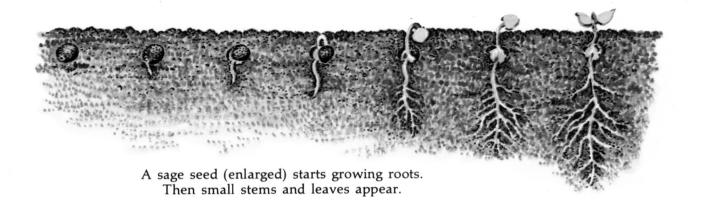

A sage seed (enlarged) starts growing roots.
Then small stems and leaves appear.

At the same time, their tiny shoots must reach the surface to get sun and air. If you plant seeds too deeply, the young sprouts may never see the sun, and they will die.

So it is best to plant only as seed packet labels direct. A light covering of soil or potting mix is usually sufficient.

Herbs take longer to sprout than most vegetables or flowers. Some may take several weeks. So you must be patient.

While you are waiting, keep the soil moist, not wet. Soon the moisture will soften the seed coatings. The first stems and leaves will begin to push through the soil, and the roots will begin to grow and take hold.

sage seedlings
(enlarged)

Seedlings

Very young plants are called seedlings. Garden stores sell seedlings. This is a quick way to start an herb garden, but it's also more expensive.

Nowadays, seedlings often come in little pots made of pressed peat moss. Just place the entire peat pot in

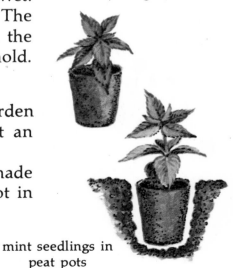

mint seedlings in
peat pots

23

Seedling ready
for transplanting.

Be sure to make
hole deep enough.

A cutting will start
to root in water.

potting mix or in the soil of your garden. Eventually, the "pot" will decay and be absorbed by the soil.

If you get seedlings in some other kind of container, remove them very carefully. Be sure to keep the soil around the roots intact.

Then place the seedlings in holes large enough for the entire root ball, and deep enough so that the root ball is about ½ inch lower than the rim of the hole.

Gently firm the soil around each seedling in its new home. Then add another ¼ inch of soil or potting mix.

Finally, put a light layer of humus or peat moss around each seedling, and water.

Cuttings

Some herbs are best started by taking cuttings from parent plants.

To make a cutting, snip off several inches of stem from the top of a mature plant. Then snip off the lower leaves of the cut-off piece. You should have about six top leaves and the tender growing tip. The rest will be just stem.

You can start cuttings in two ways:

1. Put the stems in a glass of water. When you see new rootlets begin to form, transfer the cuttings to potting soil. Firm them gently into the soil as you do with a seedling, and they, too, will take root and begin growing into new plants.

2. Or you can place cuttings immediately into potting mix. Keep the soil moist. New rootlets will form and gain a foothold. Soon, the stems will develop side shoots and begin the natural process of becoming plants.

24

Transplants

Transfering a seedling to a pot or to your outdoor garden is actually transplanting. So is digging up a grown plant and replanting it somewhere else.

But there is another way of making transplants.

Some herbs spread by sending out underground runners. These develop new stems and root systems.

To make a transplant, dig down around the stem of the new plant and carefully cut its roots away from those of the parent plant. Mint and chives are examples of herbs that can be transplanted this way.

You can use this method when you want to start a new plant or give a plant to a friend.

Gardening Tips

Save popsicle sticks. They make handy markers. With a crayon or waterproof magic marker, write the name of each herb you plant on a stick. This way, you can remember which herbs you planted in each pot or in each spot in your garden.

Another helpful trick, for both indoor and outdoor gardens: To test the soil for moisture, stick a toothpick in it, then pull it out. If the soil clings to the toothpick, it is moist enough. If the toothpick comes out dry, the herb may need water.

Follow the instructions for watering each herb in the next chapter. A general rule for herbs is that it is better to water them too little than too much.

Herbs are quite hardy. Fussing with them too much can sometimes do more harm than good.

25

underground runner
of a mint plant

Cut off a
small plant with
its roots to make
a transplant.

Popsickle sticks
make good markers.

AND NOW FOR THE HERBS!

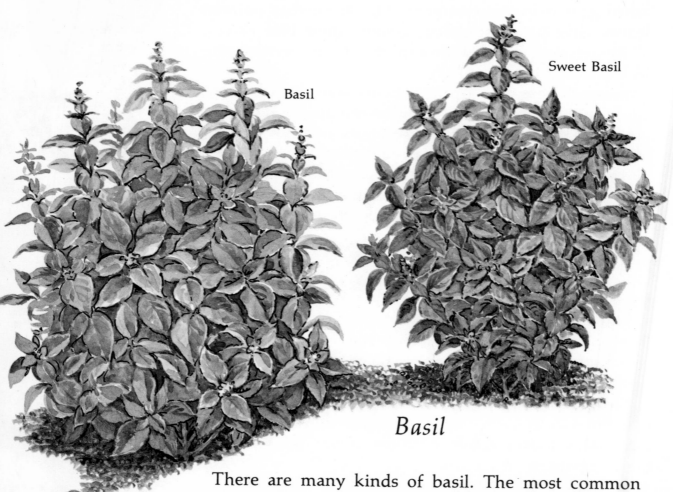

Basil

Sweet Basil

Basil

There are many kinds of basil. The most common one is sweet basil. It is called that because it has fragrant leaves for flavoring.

Basil is an annual and won't last through cold winters. It is a low-growing plant, and can be kept for months on a kitchen windowsill.

How to Know It

Basil grows 1 to 2 feet tall, usually staying smaller when grown in pots indoors. The somewhat pointed leaves have a sharp, spicy flavor, rather like cloves. They are light green with a purple tinge beneath the leaf surface.

Some varieties of basil have oval leaves with toothed edges. Others have more curly or rounded leaves.

Sweet basil has shiny green leaves about 1 to 2 inches long. White flowers appear on spikes at the end of stems in summer. But if you pinch the growing tips to use the leaves and sprigs, the flowers will be delayed and the plant will become bushier.

How to Grow It

Outdoors: Sow basil seeds as soon as the ground is warm.

Prepare soil well, then sow the seeds ⅛ to ¼ inch deep, about 1 inch apart. If you have more than one row, allow about 18 inches between rows. Seeds start sprouting in 15 to 20 days.

When plants are several inches high, thin them so that they are 8 inches apart. As they grow, pinch the top shoots to encourage bushier growth. This makes the plants more attractive.

basil leaf

basil flower

sweet basil flower

sweet basil leaf

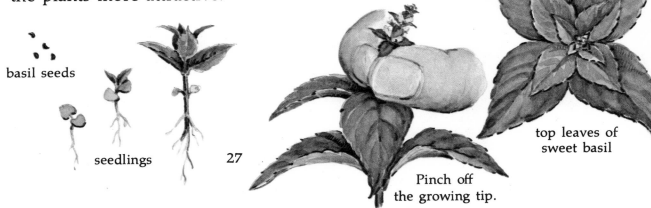

basil seeds

seedlings

Pinch off the growing tip.

top leaves of sweet basil

27

Indoors: Plant seeds any time you like. Use a 6-inch pot for 4 to 6 seeds. Space them evenly. They will grow best in a window that faces south or east, but can grow in a western window, too.

Special Care

Basil, especially sweet basil, enjoys full sun but can tolerate semishade. It likes warm, moderately rich soil.

Outdoors, water basil once a week. Indoors, keep soil moist to keep leaves plump and succulent.

Few pests bother basil. That's the beauty of herbs. They are their own best insect repellers.

How to Use It

Basil can be used to give many foods a distinctive clovelike or nutty, spicy flavor. You can use either fresh or dried leaves.

Basil is fine on cheese dishes, with fish, in stews, and in egg dishes. Basil adds a spicy taste to snap beans, cucumbers, peas, potatoes, spinach, squash, and green salads. It is most often used and is especially tasty with tomato dishes, or with spaghetti and other Italian foods.

Use fresh basil leaves whole or snip with scissors.

How to Store It

Hang a spray of basil to dry in a cool, dry room. When it is thoroughly dry, remove the leaves, crumble them, and store them in an airtight glass jar to preserve their unique aroma and flavor.

Or you can strip leaves off the stems and freeze them whole to seal in their flavor.

Another method is to add a little olive oil to fresh leaves, stirring to give them a light coating. Then freeze in a plastic bag or freezer container.

With basil you have a choice: fresh, frozen, or dried.

Chives

Chives are amazingly hardy herbs. Outdoors they can stand temperatures 25 degrees below freezing if you put a mulch around the plants to protect them.

Chives may stay evergreen in warm-winter areas, but will not keep growing in colder climates until spring awakens them again.

How to Know It

Chives are easily spotted. Their round, hollow, stem-like leaves look like a bunch of baby onions. Chives grow in grasslike clumps and have a mild onion flavor. Just snip off a piece of one of the hollow leaves and smell the oniony aroma.

The flowers look much like clover blossoms and are a pinkish purple.

This perennial plant may grow from 12 inches to 2 feet tall, making a lovely background for low-growing flowers in a bed or border. Indoors, in pots, chives seldom grow more than 12 inches tall.

How to Grow It

Outdoors: Sow seeds in the spring in moist soil. Plant them ⅛ inch deep, placing 1 seed every 2 inches. If you have more than one row, keep rows 12 to 18 inches apart.

Chives should then be thinned so that each bunch has 6 to 8 inches of growing room in a row.

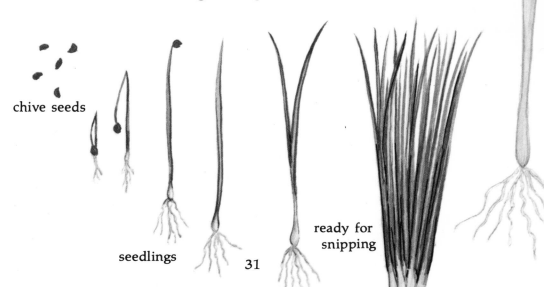

leaves

flower

chive seeds

seedlings

ready for snipping

31

You can also divide grown plants to start new ones. Simply dig up a small clump of roots and replant into a pot or new location in your garden.

Whenever you want some chives for salads, soups, or stews, just snip off the tops with scissors, and more leaves will begin growing from the mother clump. But don't cut lower than 4 inches from the base, or you will weaken the plants.

Indoors: Put 4 to 6 seeds in a 6-inch pot; space them evenly. Keep the pot near a southern or eastern window. With enough sun, chives will grow indoors all through the year.

Special Care

Chives grow well in fairly rich soil, full sun, and moist growing conditions.

Water chives regularly, at least once a week. Their hollow stems are juicy, so they need more water than most herbs. You have to replace the moisture they lose when you snip off the leaves. Misting with a light spray of water twice a week also helps to give them the extra moisture they need.

As cold weather arrives, you can pot a few clumps in clay or plastic pots to grow indoors.

How to Use It

Chives add a mild oniony flavor when snipped into salads and soups. A few snips on cheese omelets or scrambled eggs lend a tasty touch. Try a sprinkle of chives in gravies, in stews, and on baked potatoes served with sour cream. You might even enjoy nibbling a leaf or two fresh.

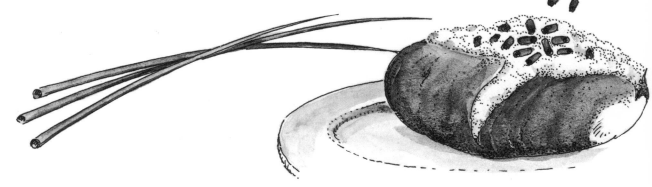

How to Store It

This herb is best used fresh. Since it thrives as a house plant, you will have plenty of it to use all year. If you wish, however, you can cut some in small pieces with scissors or a knife and store it in a plastic container in the freezer.

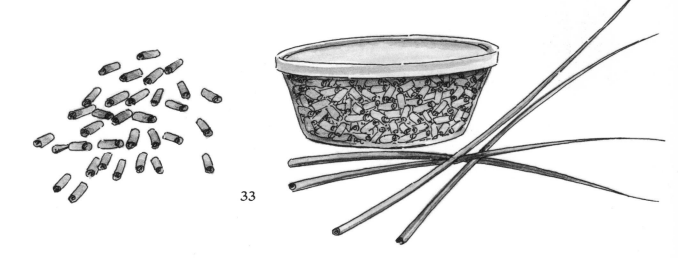

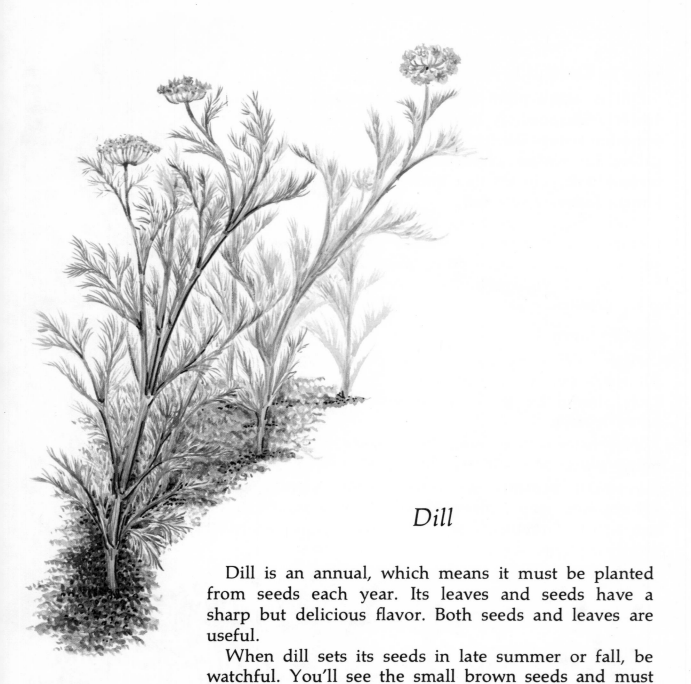

Dill

Dill is an annual, which means it must be planted from seeds each year. Its leaves and seeds have a sharp but delicious flavor. Both seeds and leaves are useful.

When dill sets its seeds in late summer or fall, be watchful. You'll see the small brown seeds and must collect them before they drop.

The umbrella-like cluster of tiny flowers is called an umbel.

How to Know It

Dill is a tall plant with finely divided leaves and flowers. The feathery light green leaves add an attractive, almost fernlike look to landscapes.

The flowers are greenish yellow and form an umbrella-shaped cluster that may grow from 3 inches to 6 inches across.

Outdoors, dill grows to 3 or 4 feet tall. Indoors as a potted plant, however, it may grow only 12 to 15 inches tall—ideal for a frilly, decorative house plant.

It will still yield plenty of leaves and seeds for use in the kitchen.

How to Grow It

Outdoors: When frost danger has passed, plant 3 to 5 dill seeds per inch, ⅛ inch deep in the garden soil. Rows should be 18 to 24 inches apart. Dill prefers sunny locations.

When the sprouts are a few inches high, thin the dill seedlings to about 5 inches apart.

Indoors: Use an 8-inch pot 10 to 12 inches deep because dill grows a deep taproot. Plant 6 to 8 seeds about 1 inch apart. Thin the seedlings, leaving only the two strongest plants. Keep near a sunny window.

leaves

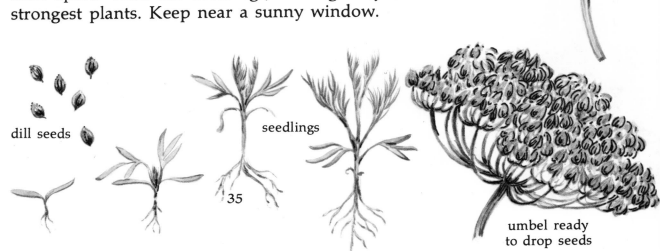

dill seeds

seedlings

35

umbel ready to drop seeds

Special Care

Because dill is slow-growing at first, keep the soil free of weeds in an outdoor garden. Outdoors, water about every other week. Indoors, once a week.

How to Use It

Dill seeds and leaves are really necessary if you want to make dill pickles. After all, that's what gives those pickles such a snappy flavor.

But dill is also used in cooking fish, chicken, lamb, and other meats. It adds flavor to gravies, sauces, and stews as well. And dill seed sprinkled on cole slaw is delicious.

It is best to use dill leaves fresh or just as the flowers open. They have a special tangy taste then. But you can cut and use dill any time after flowering begins.

How to Store It

To dry dill, cut the best leaves and place them on a clean sheet in a warm, dry spot. Leave them there for a couple of days. After the dill is thoroughly dry, crumble it and put it in an airtight glass container.

To harvest seeds, be quick. As the seeds ripen, shake the heads to release the seeds on a white sheet. They're easier to see this way. Rub them with your fingers to remove the chaff.

Store seeds in one container, crumbled leaves in another.

If you prefer to hang bunches of dill to dry, do it over a white sheet so that seeds that dry and drop out of the seed heads can be collected easily.

Fresh dill leaves can also be put in a plastic bag and stored in the freezer.

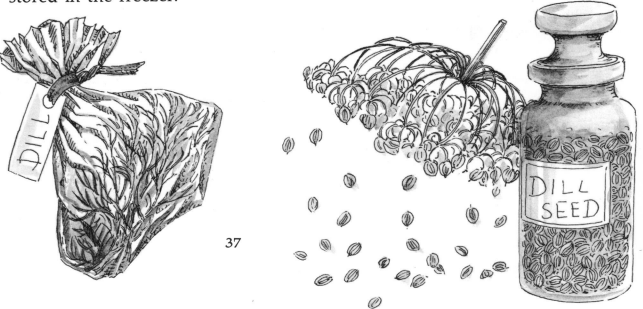

Peppermint

Spearmint

Mint

There are many types of mint. One is called apple mint because it smells and tastes like apples. Orange mint smells and tastes like oranges.

The most popular and best-known mints are peppermint and spearmint. These are the two kinds you will probably want to grow.

Mints are perennials. This means that once planted, they come up by themselves year after year.

How to Know It

Mint grows 2 to 3 feet high and has lovely small lavender or purple flowers.

All mints are easy to recognize because they have unusual square stems. But the best way to identify mint is to crush a few leaves between your fingers. If it's mint, there will be no mistaking that fresh, minty aroma.

Peppermint leaves are about 2 to 3 inches long, dark green and toothed. Spearmint has smaller leaves, also dark green, and with a crinkly feeling.

How to Grow It

Outdoors: Mint is the easiest of all herbs to grow. In fact its roots spread so rapidly it is advisable to grow mint in pots, even outdoors, to keep it under control.

Mint can be started in any of the four ways we've talked about—from seeds, from seedlings, from cuttings, and from transplants or root division. But since mint does not grow as easily from seed as other herbs, it will probably be best to start your first mints from seedlings purchased in a garden center. Or a friend may give you some from his or her garden.

leaf and flower of spearmint

peppermint leaf

mint seeds (enlarged)

All mints have square stems.

stages of growth from seed to seedling

peppermint flower

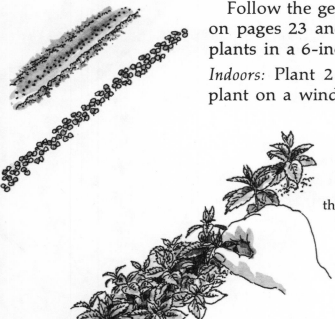

Follow the general instructions for planting seedlings on pages 23 and 24 of this book. Put no more than 3 plants in a 6-inch pot.

Indoors: Plant 2 or 3 seedlings in a 6-inch pot. Keep plant on a windowsill that faces west or north.

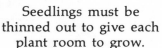

Seedlings must be thinned out to give each plant room to grow.

Special Care

Mint likes lots of moisture and partly sunny or shaded locations. Water it at least once a week, less often outdoors if there is frequent rain. Use the toothpick soil test if you are unsure. (See page 25.)

Pruning is simply snipping off the tender tips of growing plants. This makes the plant send out new side shoots and become bushier. Every time you pluck a few leaves for use in the kitchen, you are pruning the plant.

Don't pick mint leaves until your plants are at least 10 to 12 inches high. If you pick too soon, or take off too much, you may weaken the plants.

pruning

How to Use It

Mint leaves and sprigs are fun to chew.

A sprig in a cool drink of lemonade or iced tea adds a zesty flavor. Mint also makes a fine hot tea all by itself, or with just a little honey.

A few leaves added to fruit cocktails or over ice cream are both decorative and delicious.

Crushed mint leaves mixed with a little vinegar and water make a tasty homemade sauce on lamb or in stews.

Don't Store It

Mint can be grown indoors all year, and unlike most other herbs, it is best used fresh. When it is dried, it loses that special, clean refreshing taste we all enjoy.

Oregano

Oregano is a very hardy plant. It can live through freezing weather and will start growing again the next year.

This shrubby herb grows 18 to 30 inches tall. It is related to sweet marjoram and is sometimes called wild marjoram.

How to Know It

The most common variety of oregano has rounded leaves with blunt tips. The dark green leaves may be an inch or so long.

In summer, small blooms appear at the ends of the stems. These blossoms range from pinkish to almost purple.

After several years of growing, the bushy plant becomes woody. It spreads by underground runners or stems, so you can take young plants to start in new areas as you remove older bushes that have gotten too woody.

Pinching back or pruning helps keep oregano more compact. If you grow it as a potted house plant, pinching is very necessary. This will give you a more attractive, shorter, and bushier plant with tastier leaves.

How to Grow It

Outdoors: Sow oregano seeds either in early spring or late summer. Sow one seed every 3 or 4 inches, ⅛ to ¼ inch deep. Cover lightly with soil. Rows should be 18 inches apart. The seeds take 3 to 4 weeks to sprout.

flower

leaves

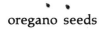

oregano seeds

seedlings

Pinch off here.

43

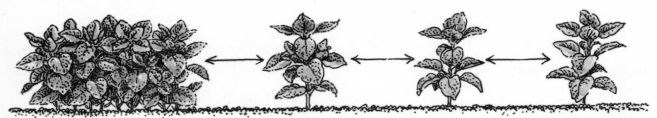

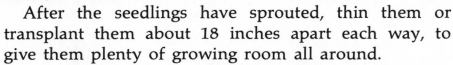

After the seedlings have sprouted, thin them or transplant them about 18 inches apart each way, to give them plenty of growing room all around.

You can also take cuttings from the top portions of fully grown plants and root them (see page 24). Use the young, tender shoots for best results. Don't use woodier parts.

Indoors: Oregano grows best in a window that faces south or east. Plant 4 to 6 seeds, spaced evenly in a 6-inch pot. When seedlings are 2 to 3 inches high, thin them, leaving only the two strongest plants.

Special Care

Oregano enjoys full sun. Water every week. For the sweetest, sharpest flavor, supply only enough water to keep the soil moist and leaves juicy and tender. Outdoors, keep a layer of humus as a mulch around your plants.

How to Use It

Oregano leaves and flower tops are used, fresh or dried, for flavoring all kinds of salads, soups, and stews.

They are good with lima beans, snap beans, eggplant, onions, peas, potatoes, spinach, and especially, tomatoes. They also add a tangy flavor to fish.

fresh leaves

dried leaves

You can hang a bunch of oregano to dry. Remove the leaves when they are dry enough to crumble.

How to Store It

Oregano can be dried like other herbs. Use only the leaves, since the stems might be woody. Spread the leaves on a clean window screen in a well-ventilated room. When the leaves are dry, crumble them and store them in sealed glass containers.

You can also freeze the leaves fresh, if you prefer. Take the leaves off the stem, put them in a plastic bag, and store in the freezer. Thaw them out when you want to put sparkle in soups, stews, and sauces.

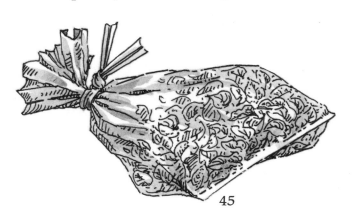

OREGANO

45

Parsley

Just about everyone has seen parsley used to garnish or decorate a plate or platter of food. Sometimes we forget it is good to eat, too.

It tastes good and is rich in vitamin C. It is also one of the easiest herbs to grow.

How to Know It

You can recognize parsley easily by its ruffled and crinkly look. This member of the carrot family is so decorative, with its finely cut toothed edges and wrinkled surfaces, that it has become perhaps the best-known "green." Yet few people realize it is an herb.

Just take a nibble and you'll discover its wonderfully fresh flavor.

How to Grow It

Outdoors: Parsley likes partly sunny to shaded growing areas. It can stand some frost, but not severe winters.

Plant parsley seeds as early as the ground can be worked. Seeds should be about 2 inches apart.

Cover the seeds with ¼ inch of soil. Rows should be 15 to 18 inches apart since parsley spreads out in a low-growing bushy pattern.

Seeds may take from 10 to 28 days to sprout, depending on the temperature of the soil, so be patient. Once the plants get started, they will grow continuously for a long time.

In rows, thin the plants so that they stand about 10 inches apart.

full-grown
parsley leaves

flower stalk

parsley seeds

seedlings

47

Just snip the sprigs you wish to use, and the plants will send up more leaves and branches. The more you cut parsley, the better it tastes.

Indoors: You can plant parsley any time indoors. It will do best on a windowsill that has western or northern exposure. If you grow it in a sunny window, set the plants back from the windowpane.

Plant 4 to 6 seeds in a 6-inch pot, evenly spaced. Do not thin the sprouts when they start coming up.

Cut off flower stalks.

Special Care

Parsley enjoys rich soil that is kept partially moist. So, for best results, water it every other day and make sure the soil is always just slightly moist.

Continue to clip or snip parsley for garnishing or flavoring. Once flower stalks form, the leaves become somewhat bitter, so keep cutting and using parsley to prevent flowering.

If you intend to keep potted plants growing all year, you should plan to use a liquid fish emulsion fertilizer every month or so. You can buy this plant food at any garden center.

How to Use It

Parsley is such a pretty herb that it is used to decorate salads, soups, and almost any dish.

But it can also flavor vegetables, meats, casseroles, soups, stews, and salads. And it is delicious chopped in poultry and egg dishes.

How to Store It

Although parsley is best used fresh, it can be frozen. Just put small bunches in plastic freezer bags and keep them in the freezer until you need them. They won't be crisp or bright green when they thaw, but they can still add color and flavor to meats and salads.

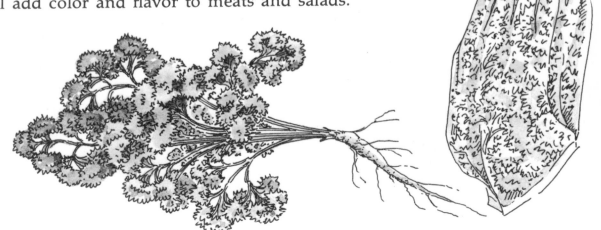

Rosemary

Rosemary is a beautiful perennial with a piney fragrance. It is hardy and grows well even in poor or dry soils.

This plant acts like a room air-freshener to give the scent of pine to your home. Outdoors, the taller varieties can be grown as hedges or shrubs. After a few years, the. stems become gnarled and woody, which adds to rosemary's eye appeal.

How to Know It

Rosemary blossoms are lavender blue, and bloom in small clusters during spring and summer. The shiny, needlelike leaves sprout all around the upright stalks or stems and resemble the needles of a pine or spruce branch.

Rosemary grows 2 to 5 feet tall, depending on the variety. In pots or containers, of course, rosemary is smaller than it would be in an outdoor garden.

How to Grow It

Outdoors: Rosemary is best grown from seed.

Plant seeds in a sunny location as early in spring as the ground can be dug up. Spade soil deeply because rosemary sets deep roots.

Sow seeds ⅛ to ¼ inch deep, about 1 inch apart. Allow 18 inches between rows. The seeds will start to sprout in 2 to 3 weeks. When the seedlings are 2 to 3 inches high, thin them to about 6 to 8 inches apart.

rosemary in full bloom

rosemary seeds

seedlings

leaf stalk

51

Indoors: You can start rosemary from seeds indoors in a pot or container any time.

Plant 4 to 6 seeds in a 6-inch pot. Rosemary needs sun, so keep it near a window that faces south or east.

When the sprouts are about 2 inches high, thin all but the two strongest plants.

Indoors or outdoors, pinch off the top shoots every few weeks to make the plant bushier.

Special Care

Because rosemary thrives in drier soil, water just once each week until it is 3 or 4 inches high. After that, once every 2 weeks is enough. Too much water will cause the leaves to become yellow and droop.

Actually, rosemary requires less care than many other herbs. Outdoors, a once-a-year feeding with humus or another organic fertilizer such as manure will take care of its growing needs. (You can buy packages of dry manure at a garden center.)

To repeat, too much water is the most serious problem that can trouble rosemary.

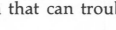

How to Use It

Rosemary can be used fresh or dried with meats, stews, and vegetables. The tender top leaves are best.

Crushed dried leaves are tangy in soups or gravies. Just a pinch in a cooking pot is enough.

You can also use a fresh sprig of rosemary to brush sauce on barbecued chicken, burgers, and ribs. It combines its tangy flavor with the sauce and gives the meat a special aroma as well.

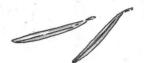

How to Store It

Rosemary can be preserved by drying.

Pick the top, tender stems on a dry summer day when the flowers are fully open. You can tie the stems together and hang them upside down in a dry room, or lay them on a clean wire window screen. Keep them as cool as possible while drying and give them good air circulation.

Then remove the leaves and store them in sealed wide-mouth jars or containers until you use them.

Sage

Sage is a distinctive herb with a pungent aroma and taste. This hardy perennial can take cold weather and snap back each year as flavorful as ever.

The fragrant, slightly bitter taste of sage comes from its leaves. Sage has a history of being useful for medicinal purposes. Whether this is true or not, its bouquet and the taste it gives to food rank it as a most popular herb.

How to Know It

This bushy shrub is about 2 feet tall when it is fully grown and has lavender or white flowers. Its long oval leaves, which may range from a few inches long to nearly 4 inches, are grayish green and somewhat coarsely textured.

Members of the sage family include the tricolor type with white and purplish leaves; golden sage with yellow variations on leaf edges; and that variety famed in song and story, the purple sage with reddish to purple foliage. These varieties are decorative in a garden but are not used as herbs.

How to Grow It

Outdoors: Sage prefers dry soil in full sun.

Plant sage seeds about ¼ inch deep, placing 2 or 3 seeds per inch. Rows should be spaced 24 to 36 inches apart. Early spring planting is best.

Sage seeds take 3 to 4 weeks to sprout.

Thin the seedlings to stand at least 10 inches apart. Since these plants start slowly, spread a 2-inch layer of humus around the plants to keep weeds under control. As sage blossoms, simply cut back the woody stems, and new branches will form to provide more leaves for your use.

full-grown leaf

blossom

flower spike

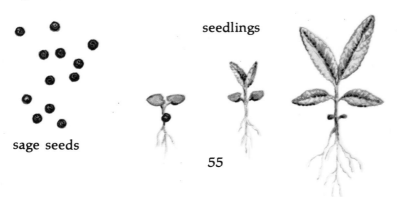

seedlings

sage seeds

55

Indoors: Sage will grow best in a sunny window—one that faces south or east. Plant 4 to 6 seeds in a 6-inch pot, evenly spaced.

When the sprouts are about 2 inches high, thin them, leaving only the two strongest plants.

Special Care

Sage, as we know from the tales of the Old West, requires little water. Outdoors, twice-a-month sprinkling in addition to natural rainfall is fine. If it rains a lot, it won't need the extra watering.

Sage can grow very well without much attention. On the other hand, too much watering can kill sage. So indoors or outdoors, don't water unless the soil is really dry.

Outdoors, a 2-inch mulching with humus early each spring can help keep sage growing nicely when you cut and use it regularly.

How to Use It

Sage leaves, fresh or dried, are a basic ingredient in stuffings and sausage and a popular meat flavoring, especially with lamb and poultry.

Sage adds a piquant or sharp taste to vegetables. It is used mostly with beans of all types, peas and tomatoes, as well as in soups and stews made with these vegetables.

How to Store It

Sage can be cut and hung in sprays to dry, or you can simply strip the leaves from the stems and spread them on a clean window screen in a warm, dry, ventilated room. Leave them there until the leaves are crisp and brittle. Then crush them and store in an airtight glass jar.

57

Sweet Marjoram

This tender, sweet-smelling herb thrives as a perennial in southern areas but must be replanted each year as an annual in colder northern climates.

Its sweet aroma and flavor were supposedly bestowed upon it by Greek goddesses.

How to Know It

In warm climates sweet marjoram is a perennial and grows between 12 and 24 inches tall—smaller, of course, in pots indoors. In areas where winters are cold, it is an annual.

Leaves are oval in shape, and grow in an opposite pattern along the stalk. Its stems branch upward.

Marjoram looks much like its relative, oregano, but its leaves are smaller.

flower
spike

How to Grow It

Outdoors: Sweet marjoram may be grown from seeds or cuttings. It needs a sunny location.

Plant 5 to 7 seeds per inch only ⅛ inch deep in late spring when the soil is well warmed. Rows should be about 18 inches apart. The seeds may take several weeks to start sprouting.

About 4 to 6 weeks after planting, thin the seedlings so that they stand 6 to 8 inches apart.

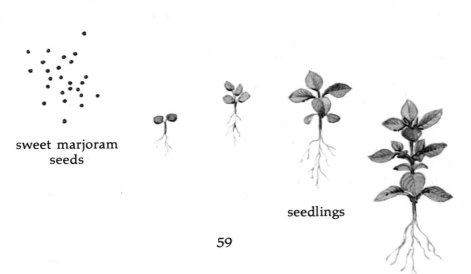

sweet marjoram
seeds

seedlings

full-grown leaves

When you add mulch, be careful not to cover the tiny seedlings.

Put cuttings in water to start roots before planting.

As with all slow-sprouting seeds, there is a danger of weeds crowding out the tiny plants. Use a 2-inch mulch of humus to keep the weeds from growing. This will also provide nutrients for the herbs.

To start from cuttings, follow the directions on page 24.

Indoors: Sprinkle the tiny seeds evenly in a 6-inch pot. Sweet marjoram will grow best in a window that faces south or east.

When the seedlings are about 2 inches high, thin out the weaker plants to give the others room to grow.

Special Care

Sweet marjoram is one of the few herbs that like alkaline (non-acid), or "sweet," soil. Because of this, you should add a little lime around each plant in the spring and again in the fall, to keep the soil alkaline. Lime is powdered limestone. You can buy it in bags at a garden center.

Marjoram prefers moist soil and full sun, so water weekly and keep soil moist for best growing.

Watch your plants. If leaves and plants look small and poor, try adding a little more lime around plants or along rows and water well. Lime takes time to dissolve and get into the soil, but bit by bit you can achieve the "sweet" soil that sweet marjoram needs.

It may be better to grow marjoram away from other herbs so that its special soil needs can be taken care of easily without changing growing conditions for the other plants.

Prune the plants regularly, every 2 weeks or so, to keep them from spreading. Cut off blossoms. This gives the leaves a better taste.

How to Use It

Pick sweet marjoram leaves any time for fresh use in salads, casseroles, or in making herbal tea. You can also use the leaves to season meats and stews, or to flavor soups with a touch of their sweet bouquet.

For a seasoning to pep up vegetables, try adding sweet marjoram to beans, carrots, eggplant, peas, and spinach.

How to Store It

You can grow sweet marjoram indoors to have fresh leaves for use all year. But the branches can also be cut and dried by hanging small bunches in a dry, warm room. Or you can spread the branches on a clean window screen in a well-ventilated dry place.

When the leaves are crisp, strip them from the stems and put them away, whole or chopped, in airtight jars for later use.

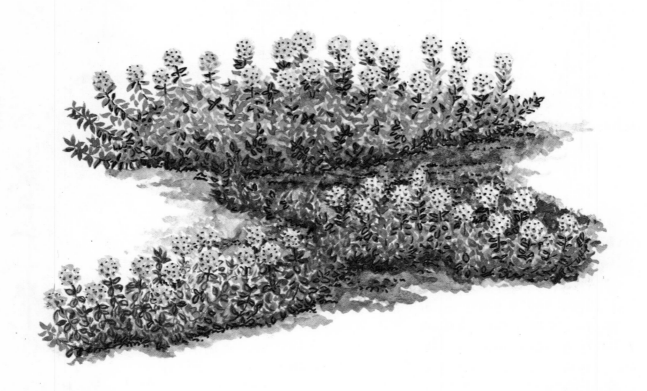

Thyme

Thyme is a shrubby, low-growing perennial with a spreading habit. It will grow well even in temperatures as low as 20 degrees below freezing. That means it can grow in all areas of the country.

Thyme is a fragrant plant. In ancient times it was thought to be the herb of happiness and courage.

How to Know It

Thyme's leaves grow along its upright stalks in an opposite pattern. That is, every leaf has another leaf directly opposite it on the stalk. Flowers appear at the ends of the stalks on spikes.

There are many varieties of thyme. Silver thyme, for example, has green and silver leaves. Lemon thyme has green leaves and a lemony fragrance.

All varieties of thyme are low-growing. Even when fully grown, some of the largest may be no taller than 12 inches.

How to Grow It

Outdoors: Thyme can be grown from seeds or cuttings. It thrives in moderately dry, light soil with a sandy or "loamy" texture. It likes good sun.

Plant seeds early in the spring when the ground is warm. Sow seeds ⅛ to ¼ inch deep and 2 inches apart. If growing in rows, make the rows 18 inches apart.

Seeds start sprouting in 15 to 20 days. When the seedlings are 2 to 3 inches high, thin the weakest ones to make room for the stronger seedlings.

Common Thyme

Lemon Thyme

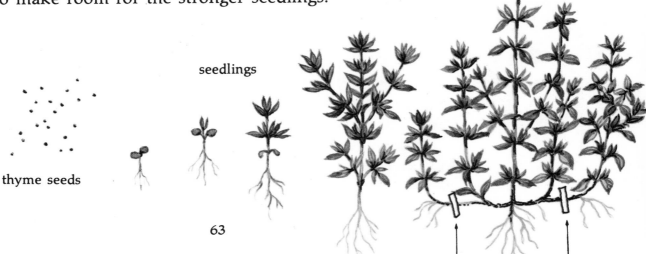

seedlings

thyme seeds

63

Cut side branches to prevent spreading.

Indoors: Sprinkle the tiny seeds in a circle in a 6-inch pot. Because thyme is so small, it is well suited to growing in pots.

Keep the pot in a window that faces south or east.

When the seedlings are 2 or 3 inches high, thin out all but the strongest plants.

Special Care

Because thyme prefers drier growing conditions, water it only every few weeks. It doesn't welcome damp roots or surroundings.

Thyme has a tendency to spread, so prune it regularly to keep it in line. Dry the parts you pinch or snip off for later use.

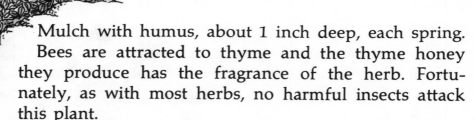

Mulch with humus, about 1 inch deep, each spring.

Bees are attracted to thyme and the thyme honey they produce has the fragrance of the herb. Fortunately, as with most herbs, no harmful insects attack this plant.

Because thyme's leaves are so tiny, their pores tend to get clogged if soot or dust are in the air. A monthly leaf-washing helps keep leaves healthy.

How to Use It

Fresh or dried, thyme adds flavor to vegetable juices, soups, and gravies. Dried, it adds a fragrant taste and aroma to fish and poultry, as well as meats. It adds a tang to sauces, too.

Thyme can be used with almost all vegetables. It goes best with lima beans, snap beans, beets, carrots, onions, potatoes, and tomatoes. The flavor of thyme is quite strong, so use it sparingly.

How to Store It

Gather thyme's leaves and stems on a dry day.

Spread them on a clean window screen or hang small bunches to dry in a warm room.

When the leaves and stems are dry, strip off the leaves and store them in airtight bottles or jars to use all season long or until your next crop is ready.

Store only the dried leaves. Discard the stems.

65

Index

Basil

Oregano

Chives

Spearmint

Dill